Boardslides in Aztlan:

A Coloring Book

Illustrated by: Marco Ramirez

For Numerous Book Orders or Speaking Engagements, please contact:

marco.photo.ramirez@gmail.com

ISBN: **978-0-578-43878-8**

This coloring book is dedicated to my parents for their unconditional support, to my mentor Kristine for her wisdom and guidance, and of course, my brother; thank you for being an amazing human.

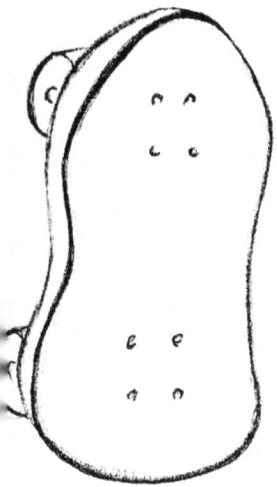

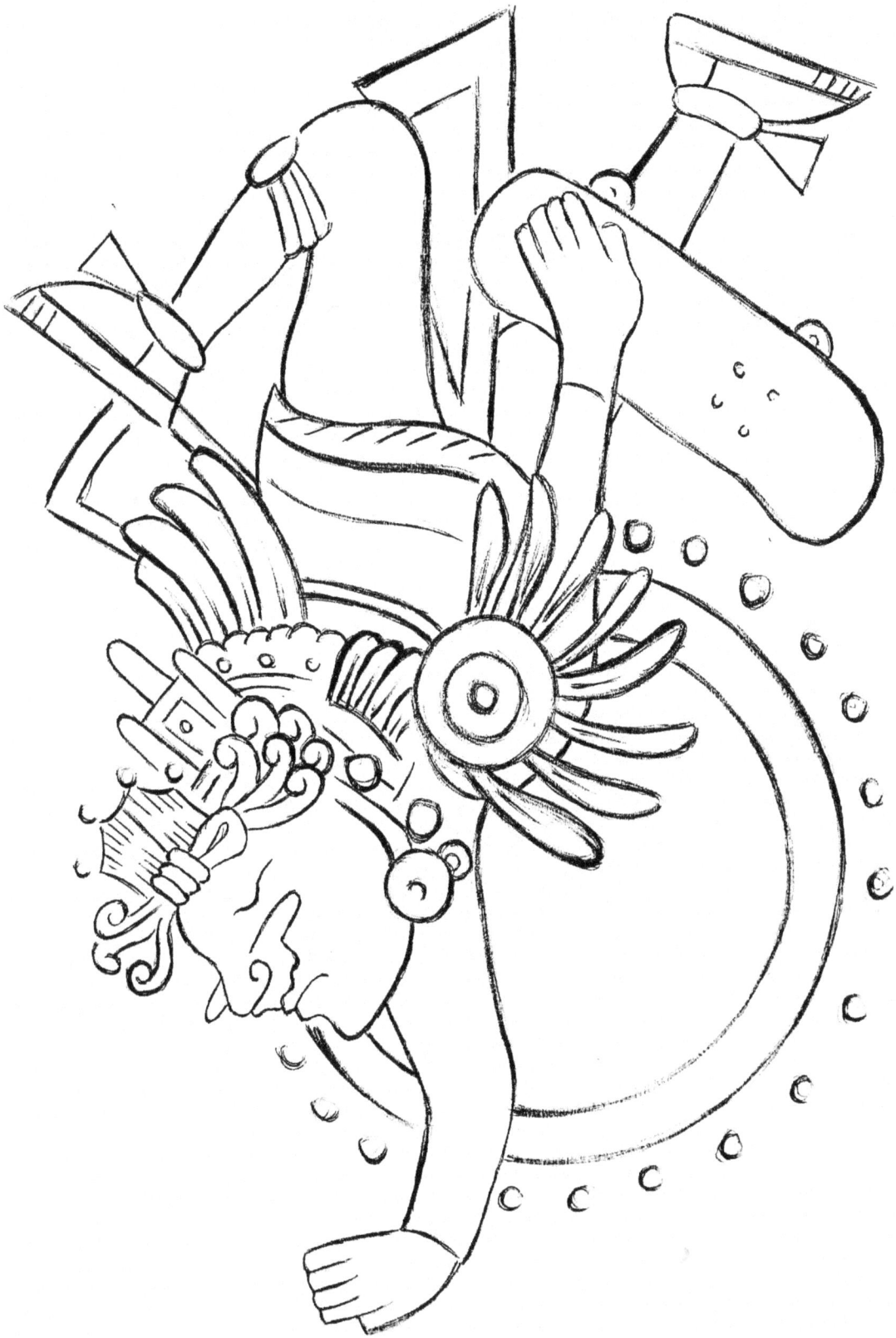

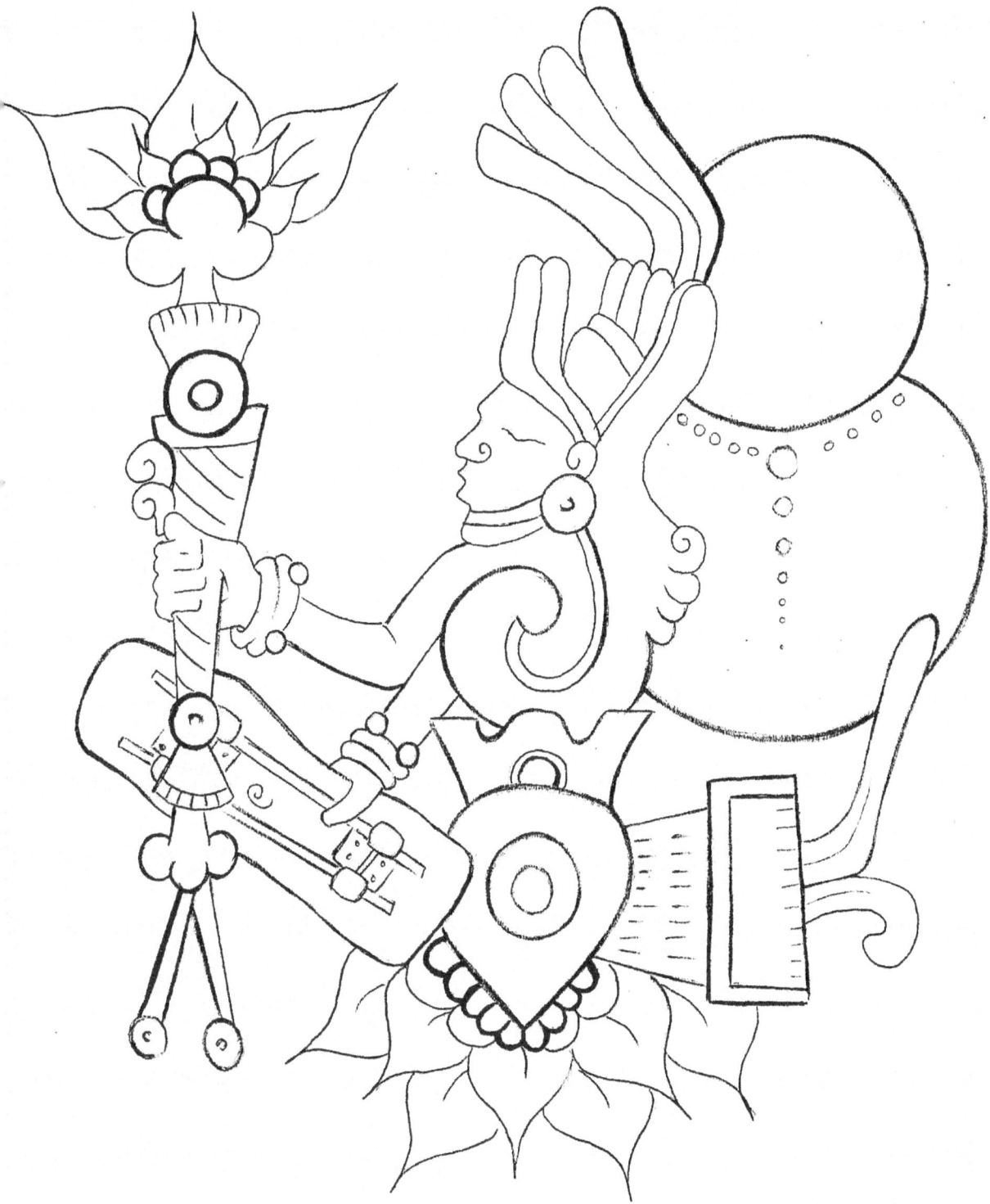